I0605908

DISCOVERING KELP FORESTS

by Charis Mather

Fusion Books, an imprint of Bearport Publishing by FlutterBee

Credits

All images are courtesy of Shutterstock.com, unless otherwise stated. Recurring – Net Vector, Baskiabat, NotionPic, PCH.Vector, LAtelier, Susann Guenther. Cover – 1000Photography, Mariia Zarai, ruppim. 2–3 – David Maki Photography. 4–5 – MVshop, F Armstrong Photography. 6–7 – Albert 1988, DR pics, Yakubovich Ekaterina. 8–9 – Damsea, Dogora Sun. 10–11 – Strannik88, valda butterworth. 12–13 – Geoff G. Wildlife Photos, Holly S Cannon, Colorcocktail. 14–15 – Greg Amptman, RLS Photo. 16–17 – jo Crebbin, LuYago, Yakubovich Ekaterina. 18–19 – Enessa Varnaeva, Joe Belanger. 20–21 – Danita Delimont, Shivram. 22–23 – DoublePHOTO studio, Damsea.

Bearport Publishing Company Product Development Team

Kayla Eggert, Theresa Emminizer, Kim Jones, Allison Juda, Cole Nelson, Naomi Reich, Steve Scheluchin, Tiana Tran

Library of Congress Cataloging-in-Publication Data is available at www.loc.gov or upon request from the publisher.

ISBN: 979-8-89577-812-8 (hardcover)
ISBN: 979-8-89577-824-1 (ebook)

For more information, write to Bearport Publishing, 3500 American Blvd W, Suite 150, Bloomington, MN 55431.
Printed in the United States of America.

CONTENTS

ALL ABOARD!

Ahoy! Are you here for the See-Gulls Ocean Tour? If so, you are in the right place. My name is Captain Gulliver, and this is my trusty **crew.**

We know about everything there is to see at sea. Today, we'll be exploring kelp forests! Keep a lookout for the animals that call these underwater jungles home.

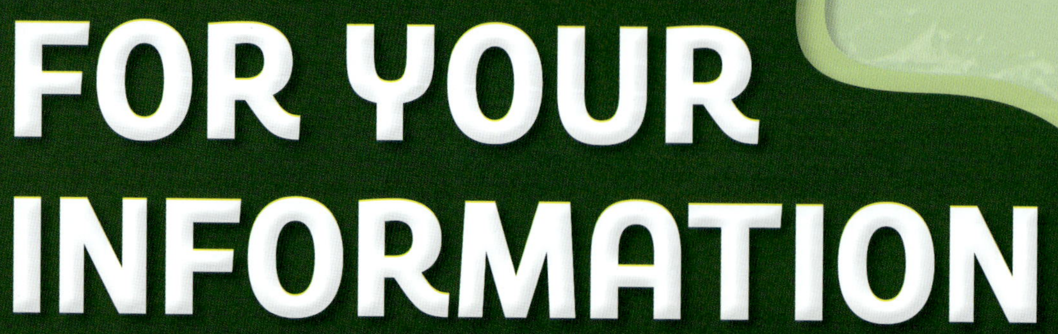

FOR YOUR INFORMATION

Kelp forests grow in cool, **shallow** waters close to the shore. They grow in thick groups, which can make it hard for boats to get through!

Don't worry! We can handle this.

These underwater forests help protect the land. When big waves roll in, the kelp stops them from hitting the coast too hard. They also create a safe place for many animals to live.

Kelp can grow up to 18 inches (46 cm) in one day.

KELP

Kelp looks and acts a lot like a plant. It needs sunlight to live and grow. And it even has parts that look like leaves and roots. But kelp is really a kind of **algae**!

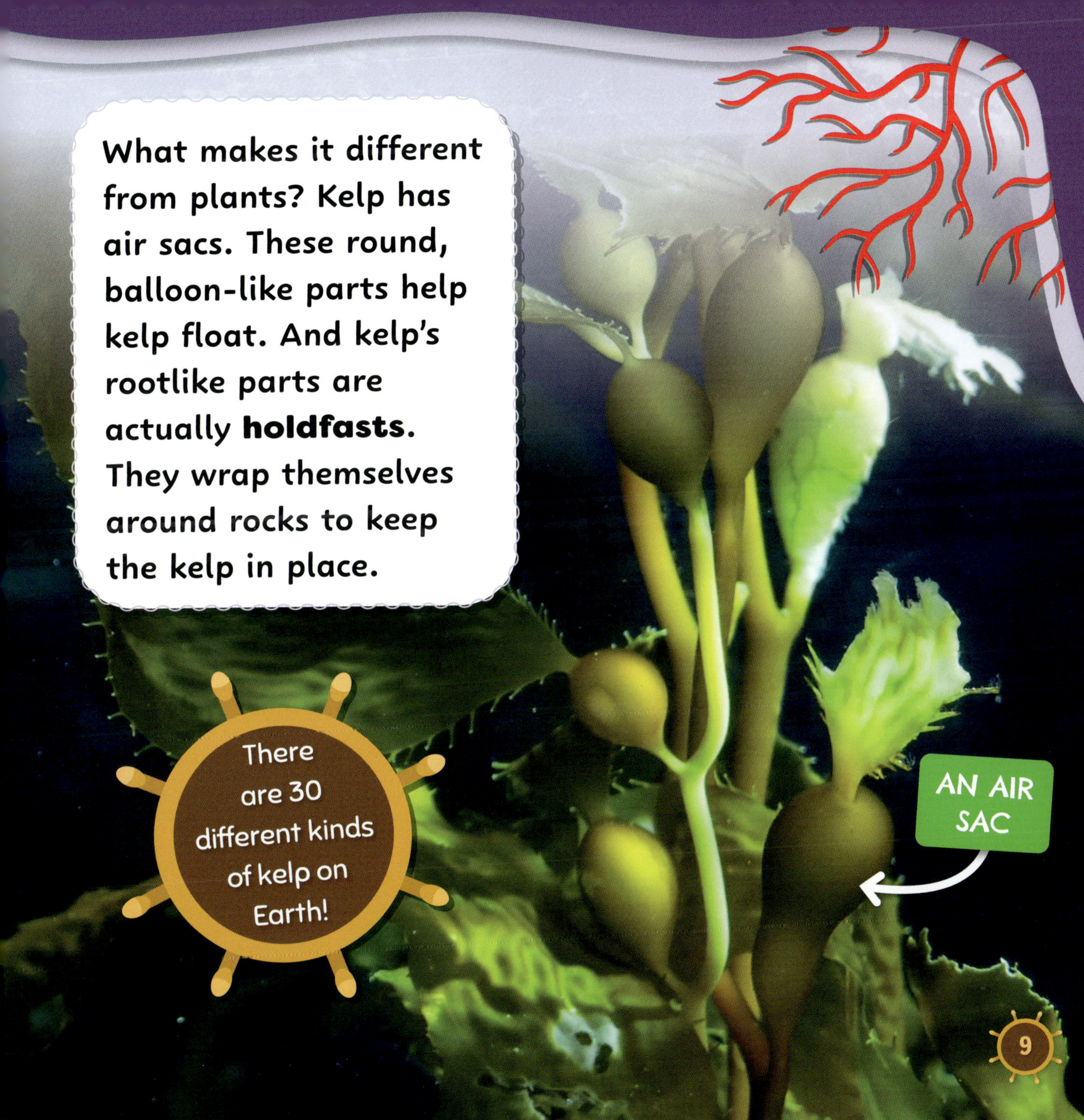

What makes it different from plants? Kelp has air sacs. These round, balloon-like parts help kelp float. And kelp's rootlike parts are actually **holdfasts.** They wrap themselves around rocks to keep the kelp in place.

SEA URCHINS

Kelp forests are good places to find sea urchins. Most sea urchins are small, round, and covered in spines. These animals are often brightly colored, which makes them easy to spot.

Don't step on a sea urchin. Those spines hurt!

A SEA URCHIN

But sea urchins can be harmful to kelp forests. They eat through the kelp's holdfasts. Without these, the kelp drifts away in the waves.

Sea urchins can't swim! They use their tubelike feet to slowly move along the ocean floor.

SEA OTTERS

Sea otters help keep the kelp forest healthy by eating sea urchins. The cute, furry animals also eat crabs. Sea otters catch these creatures with their paws and bring them up to their mouths to nibble on.

Sea otters have thick, oily fur that helps them stay warm in cold waters.

When sea otters rest, they wrap themselves in kelp. This stops the animals from drifting away.

SUNFLOWER SEA STARS

It might be named after a plant, but the sunflower sea star is actually an animal. Though most sea stars have five arms, a sunflower sea star can have up to 24!

Sea stars are sometimes called starfish.

Sunflower sea stars don't have brains or eyes. They find food by sensing light and smells around them. Sunflower sea stars eat both living and dead prey.

GRAY WHALES

Gray whales swim through kelp forests. They come to eat tiny creatures called zooplankton. The whales use their brushlike **baleen** to **filter** zooplankton from the water.

Gray whales also come to kelp forests to hide from predators, such as killer whales.
How does my kelp hat look?
Sometimes, gray whales can be seen wearing kelp like a hat!

GARIBALDI FISH

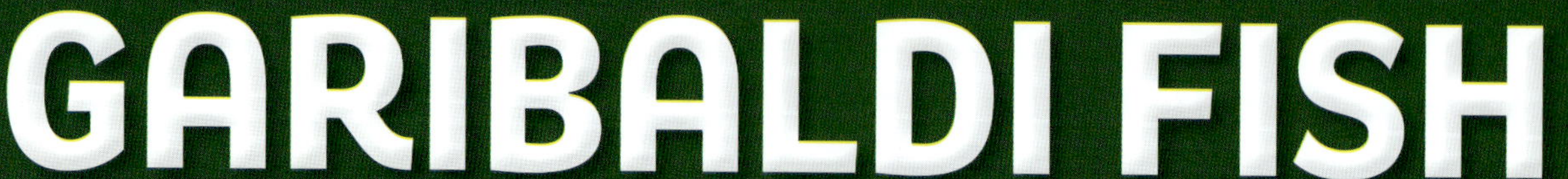

With their bright orange color and heart-shaped tails, garibaldi fish are certainly eye-catching. **Males** even swim in loops to get **females** to notice them!

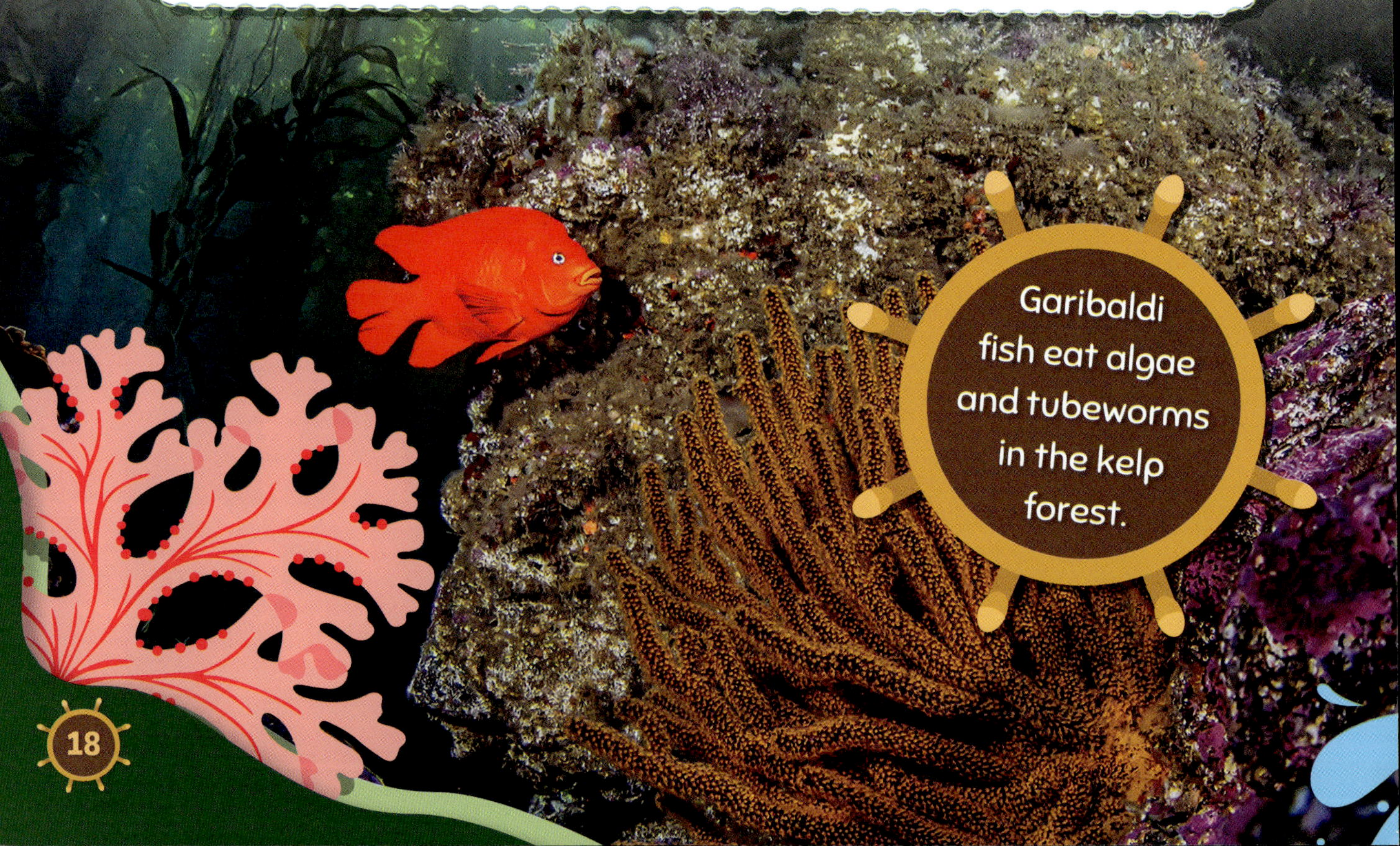

Garibaldi fish eat algae and tubeworms in the kelp forest.

Male garibaldi fish make tidy nests and invite females to lay eggs inside. Then, they guard the eggs until they **hatch**.
I think that garibaldi fish is telling us to scram!

EGRETS

Of course, our tour of the kelp forests would not be complete without sea birds. Egrets visit kelp forests to find food.

Egrets dine on fish, snails, and other animals that live in the kelp forest.

Egrets walk on the thick mats of floating kelp while looking for food below. When an egret spots prey hiding in the kelp, it spears the meal with its sharp beak.

BACK ON LAND!

We could be here all day watching the wildlife in the kelp forest, but our tour has come to an end. We hope you have enjoyed your time with us.

Come back soon to explore other parts of the ocean. There is always more to see at sea!

GLOSSARY

algae plantlike living things that are found in water

baleen part of a whale's mouth used to filter food out of the water

crew the group of people who work on a ship

females animals that can have young

filter to separate one thing from another

hatch to come out of an egg

holdfasts the parts of kelp that hold it in place

males animals that cannot have young

predators animals that hunt other animals for food

prey animals that are hunted by other animals for food

shallow not deep

INDEX